Scoots, the Bog Turtle

Scoots
the Bog Turtle

by Judy Cutchins and Ginny Johnston
illustrated by Frances Smith

ATHENEUM   1989   NEW YORK

Atheneum
Macmillan Publishing Company
866 Third Avenue, New York, NY 10022
Collier Macmillan Canada, Inc.
First Edition   Printed in Singapore

10   9   8   7   6   5   4   3   2   1

Library of Congress Cataloging-in-Publication Data
Cutchins, Judy.
Scoots, the bog turtle/by Judy Cutchins and Ginny Johnston; illustrated by
Frances Smith. —1st ed. p.   cm.
Summary: Presents a year in the life of a little bog turtle in his natural habitat.
ISBN 0-689-31440-X
1. Bog turtle—Juvenile literature.   2. Bogs—Juvenile literature.
[1. Bog turtle.   2. Bogs.   3. Turtles.]   I. Johnston, Ginny.
II. Smith, Frances, ill.   III. Title.
QL666.C584C87 1989
597.92—dc19   88-19262 CIP AC

Introduction

Bogs are rare and unusual wetlands found mostly in the eastern part of the United States. Although a bog looks like a grassy meadow with a few trees and shrubs, it is really deep mud covered by soft, spongy moss. Rain and gently trickling streams keep the bog wet all year. Each winter the moss dies back; each spring new growth turns the bog green again. As the old, dead moss decays beneath the new, the bog becomes deeper and muckier.

Unfortunately, some people think bogs are wasted areas because they cannot be farmed or built on. But wetlands are important habitats for many different living things. Some plants and animals are especially adapted for life in the unique bog habitat. The tiny bog turtle, for example, lives in no other place. If bogs are not protected from human disturbance, they will soon disappear—and so will the plants and animals that live there.

This is the story of a year in the life of a little bog turtle we named Scoots. Until recently, not much was known about bog turtles, except that they are the smallest of North American turtles and they are found only in bogs. Scoots lives in Duck Potato Bog, named for plants with arrowlike leaves, called duck potatoes.

While Scoots and Duck Potato Bog are imaginary names, all the plants and animals in the story really live in bogs of the North Carolina mountains. The story itself is a true-to-life adventure that takes place in a beautiful and mysterious wildlife habitat.

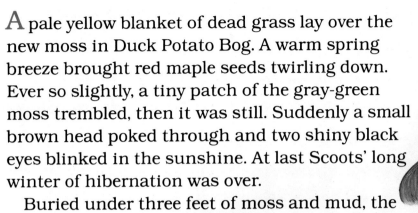

A pale yellow blanket of dead grass lay over the new moss in Duck Potato Bog. A warm spring breeze brought red maple seeds twirling down. Ever so slightly, a tiny patch of the gray-green moss trembled, then it was still. Suddenly a small brown head poked through and two shiny black eyes blinked in the sunshine. At last Scoots' long winter of hibernation was over.

Buried under three feet of moss and mud, the little bog turtle had not seen the quiet snowfalls or felt the icy storms of winter. With the coming of spring, the temperature of the earth had warmed and so had Scoots. For several days he had been gradually digging up and out of his hiding place beneath the roots of a willow tree. As soon as his head popped through the moss, Scoots stretched his neck and gulped the fresh air of April.

As he clambered out of the mud, he felt the
warmth of the sun on his chocolate-brown shell.
The soft, spongy moss squished as Scoots crawled
away from his wintering spot. He reached one of
the many small streams that crisscrossed Duck
Potato Bog. The shallow water was cold and clear
as it trickled by. Scoots put his head completely
under and took a long drink. The water made the
bright orange blotches on his head glisten in the
sunlight. He was a very handsome four-year-old
bog turtle.

Scoots climbed onto a tiny hill of grass to bask in the late afternoon sunshine. Lifting his head, he gulped the warm air for several seconds. He was gulping to smell as well as to breathe. The earthy odor of the wet bog was fresh and familiar. Scoots' keen sense of smell picked up the sweet scent of an orchid, one of the earliest flowers to bloom in Duck Potato Bog.

Before dark he left the grassy hill and dug a few inches under the moss to spend his first night out of hibernation. The night was clear and beautiful. A full yellow moon rose between the mountains, casting light on all the shallow pools. Spring peeper frogs called to each other from every part of the bog. Swift bats zigzagged through the air, hunting insects for their evening meal. High in a maple tree, a barred owl watched for movement on the ground below. She was searching for mice to feed her newly hatched youngsters. When she spotted a mouse, she swooped down on powerful wings and snatched it up with her knife-sharp claws.

All at once the spongy moss quivered, sinking and rising above Scoots' head. Something large and heavy was walking in the bog above him. It was a mother raccoon. The furry masked hunter had left her den in a tree stump to search for food. If she found Scoots, the hungry raccoon could tear him right out of his shell with her sharp teeth and claws.

Suddenly the bog was deathly silent. Then a splash and a loud croak told the story—the hungry raccoon had caught a frog. Soon the quaking bog above Scoots was still. The raccoon had moved away. Beneath the cool moss, Scoots drifted into a deep sleep.

The next morning the little turtle dug out and followed a winding thread of water as it flowed slowly through the bog. He was heading for the wettest, muckiest part, the place he had spent each of his four summers. As he journeyed, Scoots burrowed into the mud at the end of each day and stayed through the night. If the following day was warm and sunny, Scoots crawled out of the mud and continued on his way. He traveled only forty or fifty feet each day. Plowing through the thick tangle of grass and moss was slow, hard work for a three-inch turtle.

As Scoots followed the gently trickling stream, the water became a few inches deeper. Floating in the water was a baseball-sized glob of clear jelly. Inside the glob were dozens of wiggly black leopard frog tadpoles. Scoots ripped into the hatching egg mass. Hungrily, he swallowed mouthfuls of the slippery tadpoles.

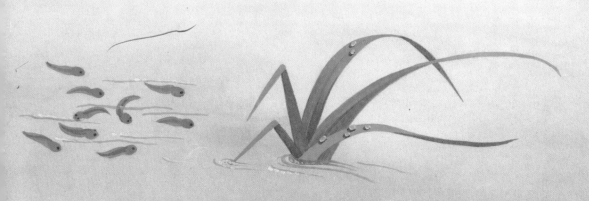

The water was just over Scoots' head as he moved along, sometimes walking on the muddy bottom and sometimes carried by the slow-moving water. At last, one week after coming out of hibernation, Scoots was in the middle of Duck Potato Bog. It was the perfect place for a bog turtle to spend the summer. With his sharp, strong claws, Scoots could dig quickly into the mud to hide whenever he was surprised or startled.

The water was fresh, clear, and cold. It trickled steadily downhill as the snow on the mountain-tops melted. The flat bog held water like a giant saucer. Hundreds of little grass clumps were scattered all over it. Scoots could dig under the grass roots or climb up on the clumps to bask in the sunshine. The dead leaves and grass that lay like a mat over the surface of the bog were home to snails and slugs, two of Scoots' favorite meals.

Dead moss and leaves of earlier years had decayed into soil. The seeds of bog plants took root in it and sprouted. As the plants grew, they towered over Scoots' head and made a maze of shadows on the ground. Scoots' shell, with its pattern of orange, blended in with the shadows and camouflaged the little turtle when he was basking.

A jungle of rhododendron and a thicket of prickly sticker vines kept some of Scoots' deadly enemies, like foxes and skunks, from moving quietly through the bog to hunt.

Fuzzy white flowers on the silky willow attracted bees and butterflies to the bog. Many of the insects that fell into the water were gobbled up by the hungry bog turtle. The layers of moss Scoots clambered across were the rooftops of tunnels and runways made by mice and voles.

The weather grew warmer as spring made way for summer. The days were peaceful and quiet, interrupted only by the shrieks of blue jays, the rat-a-tat-tat of woodpeckers, and the steady buzzing of the insects that lived in Duck Potato Bog. Scoots remained safely hidden beneath the cool mud for hours at a time while the bog was alive with activity all around him.

Finding or catching food is the chief occupation of the bog animals, no matter how large or small they are. The mouselike meadow vole moved quickly among the grassy clumps in search of seeds and new green plants. She stopped often to watch and listen for enemies. The hungry hawk from the forest nearby circled the bog looking for snakes and small mammals, like the vole.

In a shallow pool, a big brown fishing spider rested on a floating leaf. Two of its eight legs touched the water, feeling for ripples made by any insect that might land in the pool. It was not long before a thirsty fly flew in for a drink. The spider's velvety feet made dimples on the surface as the swift hunter skated after its victim. The venom in the spider's bite poisoned the insect. Then the spider carried the fly back to the leaf and slowly ate the insect meal.

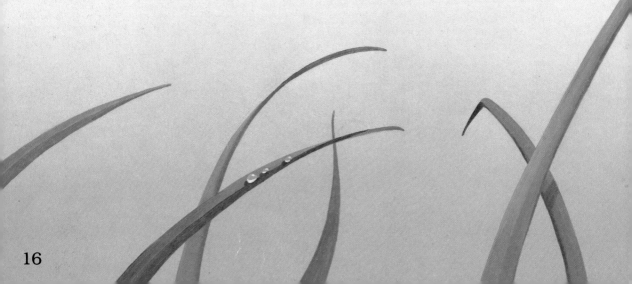

Scoots climbed out of the pool and onto a grassy
island. He was hungry. Using his sharp eyesight,
he spotted a caterpillar that had fallen into the
shallow water. With astonishing speed, the bog
turtle lunged back into the pool. He stretched his
neck as long as it would reach. With one quick
movement, Scoots grasped the wiggling larva. In
just a few seconds, he had swallowed the
caterpillar whole.

A long-legged heron flapped in and landed in the mud near Scoots. Instantly, Scoots pulled his head as far into his shell as it would go. He tucked his legs and tail close to his body, but he could not close up tight inside his shell the way some turtles do. He heard the stab as the heron speared a green frog with a lightning-fast jab of its sharp beak. Unlike the frog, Scoots had nothing to fear from the heron now that he had grown. His three-inch shell was too large and hard for the heron's beak.

One morning Scoots saw large, dark clouds reflected in a pool. By noon the sky over Duck Potato Bog had turned to a deep purple-gray. A cool breeze began to stir the leaves of the willows. Scoots gulped the air. He could smell rain and feel the cooler temperature. He dug down under the mud to wait out the approaching storm. The sound of thunder rumbled louder. Birds fluffed up their feathers as they nestled closer to tree trunks. A queen snake dropped onto the moss from a low alder branch and slithered under a rotting log. Then the bog was pounded by rain pouring from the dark clouds. Moss swelled like a sponge as it soaked up the raindrops. The summer storm lasted all afternoon.

As twilight approached, the storm ended. The bog was cool and dripping and peaceful. Sounds of the storm had stopped and night sounds of the bog were beginning. The voices of frogs and the shrill chirps of crickets cut through the peace and quiet.

That night every pool seemed to come alive with hungry salamanders. They crawled from under roots and logs. In the damp darkness, they searched for insects to eat. Their slippery bodies marched over the wet moss as the moonlight danced across their backs.

21

The next morning a mist rose from the bog as the sun gradually warmed the earth. Scoots dug out early to catch the sun on his shell before the day got too hot. Just as he stretched his legs and found the perfect spot for basking, he froze. There, a few inches away, a giant snapping turtle lay motionless in the mud. It was as big around as a dinner plate and probably weighed twenty pounds. Many a tiny bog turtle has been gobbled up in a single bite of a snapper. Scoots could see the wide head and the jaws that were powerful enough to break a turtle's shell. The snapping turtle had not seen the little bog turtle. Flipping tail-up, Scoots went down headfirst into the soft mud. With tiny legs flailing, he was safely buried in seconds.

Staying beneath the mud was no problem for Scoots. He did not have to hold his breath. He had a special way of breathing when he was under water or wet mud. Under his tail, Scoots' body has an opening called a cloaca. When water is pulled into the cloaca, oxygen from the water passes through the thin skin right into his bloodstream.

Nearly an hour later Scoots slowly dug out of the safety of the mud. Sticking his head up first and looking cautiously around, he found that the snapper was no longer in sight. The little turtle plowed over new, fuzzy fronds of a cinnamon fern and made his way to the soft mud under an alder shrub. There he dug just an inch into the mud, leaving the top of his shell exposed to the sun's warming rays.

In the cool morning after the storm, plants that had drooped from the pounding rain were standing tall again. Colorful copper butterflies and buzzing honeybees were attracted to the sweet fragrances and juicy nectar of the bog flowers.

For insects, certain sweet-smelling plants are deadly. One of these is the pitcher plant. It has pretty striped green leaves and a heavy odor of perfume. Scoots looked up just in time to see a bee land on the mouthlike leaf of a pitcher plant. When the bee went inside to collect the sweet nectar, its feet slid on a waxy, slippery layer. The bee fell into the liquid at the bottom of the pitcher. Buzzing and struggling, the insect tried to escape. But it was trapped. The bee drowned and was gradually digested by the juices of the insect-eating pitcher plant.

As the summer moved along, finding food grew easier for Scoots. Insects seemed to be everywhere. They were flying, crawling, and swimming all through the bog. One morning Scoots went after a damselfly that had landed on a grassy island. But Scoots did not have a chance to catch the insect. It flew away, startled by another turtle that looked like Scoots. It was a female bog turtle that had mated with a male turtle early in the spring. Now she was making a nest for her eggs in the grassy mound. The soil there was soft and not very wet. The mother bog turtle carefully shoveled up little bits of dirt with her back claws. Soon she had made a bowl-shaped hole in the soil. Crawling over the opening, the mother bog turtle laid five chalky white eggs. Then she covered the eggs with soil. Afterward she crawled away, not noticing Scoots at all. The mother turtle would never return to her eggs. The summer's warmth would incubate them and they would hatch in the fall.

As the sunny days grew longer and hotter,
Scoots remained buried in the cool mud most of
each day. The brown spider hid from the sun's
rays beneath a fallen leaf. Snakes ventured out
to eat only after sunset.

Each evening the barred owl flew over the bog in
search of small mammals. Her babies grew strong
on their diet of mice and insects. Soon the young
owls left the nest to live alone. Young raccoons
played at night and followed their mother as she
taught them to hunt.

At last, just like every year before, the summer
days became shorter. Scoots could sense the cooler
temperatures as fall approached.

By late fall life in the bog had changed noticeably. Titmice and chickadees chirped excitedly on cold mornings. It was time for birds to migrate to a warmer place. The old snapping turtle settled deep beneath the mud for the winter. Trees dropped their colorful leaves and the green ferns turned brown. The sun was no longer high in the afternoon; it cast long shadows across the bog. Even the air smelled different as Scoots took in big gulps. Before the weather became too cold, Scoots headed back along the little stream to the place he had hibernated each winter of his life. He dug deep into the mud beside the old willow.

When winter arrived, temperatures fell below freezing. The sky often filled with clouds so thick and heavy they looked as though they might fall right into Duck Potato Bog. Snow fell, burying the once green bog in a thick cover of white. It would be months before Duck Potato Bog was warm and green again. Until then, Scoots would stay safely tucked away three feet deep beneath the roots of the old willow.

Index